M
of the Cosmos

Explore the Mystery of Melanin, Black Civilization, and Melanated Beings as it Relates to the Universe.

© **Copyright 2018 - All rights reserved.**

The contents of this book may not be reproduced, duplicated or transmitted without direct written permission from the author.

Under no circumstances will any legal responsibility or blame be held against the publisher for any reparation, damages, or monetary loss due to the information herein, either directly or indirectly.

Legal Notice:

You cannot amend, distribute, sell, use, quote or paraphrase any part or the content within this book without the consent of the author.

Disclaimer Notice:

Please note the information contained within this document is for educational and entertainment purposes only. No warranties of any kind are expressed or implied. Readers acknowledge that the author is not engaging in the rendering of legal, financial, medical or professional advice. Please consult a licensed professional before attempting any techniques outlined in this book.

By reading this document, the reader agrees that under no circumstances are is the author responsible for any losses, direct or indirect, which are incurred as a result of the use of information contained within this document, including, but not limited to, —errors, omissions, or inaccuracies.

Introduction

What is it about the sun that comforts us in a way similar to none? That natural force that awakens you from unconscious. Those warm sunrays piercing the sky, gleaming down on your body in a positive frequency. That natural calm that occurs when you take a moment to appreciate the universe as you raise self-awareness. The cool breeze that passes over your shoulder and puts you at ease with your surroundings. We are creatures of light, love, and peace. Within us lies the information of the universe, a sweet sacred element known as melanin.

Melanin has numerous health benefits for the body, but it also exists on a cosmic level. This sacred element is found in small amounts in every creation, even inanimate objects. People who possess concentrated amounts of melanin are advantaged when exposed to the sun. Melanated beings are vibrant creatures deeply rooted in the cosmos, known for living in harmony with nature, they are the original beings of the Earth.

Melanin is a chemical produced by the pineal gland of the brain. Through autopsies performed on deceased soldiers during the Vietnam War, it was learned that the pineal gland of the brain is larger in African Americans. The darker pigment of skin is a result of the melanin- but many more discoveries are known.

Melanin exists as a powerful spiritual energy. It is much more than just the pigment of one's skin color; melanin is also the core fundamental unit that makes up the entirety of the universe. It emits and absorbs energy, works in the brain, and digest information from sunlight. Melanin makes you more receptive to all the energy sources on the light spectrum, much more than a person lacking this element. This is because the color white is naturally reflective and pushes away all light while black, the color of melanin, absorbs all light.

It is this ability to absorb and see the entire spectrum of light that makes melanated beings unique. By seeing and emitting all the lights on the spectrum, they access heightened creativity and knowledge of the universe. Recent studies have shown that light actually carries within it intelligent information. When you receive sunlight, you are essentially downloading and converting new information from the universe. You can charge this energy and help it flow, while giving you greater ideas and enlightened perspective. Melanin, therefore, is a driving power of the universe and connects to us all both physically and energetically.

As you read this book, you will unlock the knowledge to increase and understand your identity. You will learn how to increase the melanin contained in your body and exponentially, your abilities to attract what you desire in life. You will also learn about what to avoid in regards of nutrition, and how melanin exists on a cosmic level.

Enjoy! Keep your mind open to the pure, fulfilling life that you can lead as you learn the key components of light, love, and energy.

Chapter 1: What is Melanin?

Most people know melanin only as its physical manifestation, as it is the presence of melanin within a person that determines how light or dark their skin tone is. However, it is also much more. It is the dark matter present in every being in the universe, existing on even a cellular level. It is the core unit of existence with the power to emit and absorb energy. It also improves digestive function, vision, and the inner workings of the brain. Produced by the pineal gland, it is still found in every organ in the human body, flowing through the blood and being present in every subatomic particle of the body.

The purest form of melanin is black because it absorbs all colors. It is found in the eyes, hair, and skin of people of African descent in varying degrees. The darker that the melanin is, the more concentrated it has taken form.

Melanin: What Does it Mean?
Melanin, like most words, can be broken down into its origins to form an understanding of the

full term. The first part of the word, 'MEL' is derived from the Greek word Milano, which means black. 'ANIN' is derived from the word Amine, which describes a functional group with a nitrogen base and additional hydrocarbons. Therefore, melanin means 'black amine.'

This definition makes sense, because melanin is black in its purest form. This is because melanin works like any other thing seen by the human eye. For the human eye to see color, it is captured as reflections from light. Only when light is reflected from the surface of an object or a being will there be color. When a surface has no color and reflects no light, it appears black in color. Melanin cells, when in their purest form, have absorbed a large amount of energy. Since melanin never loses that energy once it becomes pure, it will always remain black.

Now, it has been described that melanin is black in its purest form. But what about when it is not pure? Melanin is a pigment. As a pigment, it has varying shades that can exist in the human body. Melanin can be tinted anywhere on the spectrum from yellow to pure black. It is most often yellow-tinted in Caucasian and Asian people and exists in its purest form in those with a dark skin color and a rich African heritage.

ABOUT PINEAL AND MELANIN (The Science)

Interestingly melanin absorbs all types of energy such as sunlight, electromagnetic, music heard by the human ear and sounds the human ear cannot hear, phone waves, radio waves, radar, computer radiation, x-ray, cosmic rays, ultraviolet rays, heat waves, microwaves, etc. Very similar to the expression, *"You are what you eat and listen to."* Melanin uses the energy in the entire universe such as water energy, earth, moon, sun, galaxy, cycles of planets, cycles of minerals etc. On the molecular level the melanin particles called electrons, protons, neutrons and solitons rearrange their orbit. This is called resonance. In other words, the melanin particles vibrate and rearrange themselves to fill the weak (low) energy sites. Resonance causes a particle to move, this movement causes a small gap (low energy) site and the other particles rearrange themselves to (double bond shift) fill the gap.

Melanin is the natural chemical that makes Black people's skin Black. It is present in Black people's bodies, skin, cells, nerves, brain, muscles, bones, reproductive and digestive systems and all bodily functions in a higher amount than all other races.

Melanin is a biological active substance of various size cells. It is made of nutrients such as indoles, histamines, phenylalanine, catecholamines (norepinephrine, epinephrine, dopamine, etc.) and the amino acid tyrosine. Melanin is made of various attached parts called chains which are linked to unsaturated carbon-carbon, saturated carbon-carbon, carbon-nitrogen, organometallic, ether. Peroxides and quinine which are brown to black in color. Chemicals such as Flavin, Pteridines, Flavonoid, Naphthoquinone, Polycyclic Quinone, Anthraquinone, Phenoxazine, convert into Melanin (polymerize or co-polymerize).

The color of melanin appears as black because it is absorbing all colors. Once the color enters the melanin it cannot escape. Melanin is concentrated colors, it is a cellular Black Hole similar to the Black Holes in outer space. The human eye only sees colors that are reflected away from an object. If an object appears Black in color, that means that the object is absorbing all colors except Black. Black is reflected away from the object, consequently, you see Black. Black is a pigment (color) that makes carbon Black in appearance.

Melanin on a Scientific Level:

Melanin is synthesized (produced) by the body when the chemical L-3, 4-dihydroxyphenylalanine is catalyzed by tyrosine. The amino acid tyrosine is the key to this process. Tyrosine is both produced by the body and can be supplemented with pills or naturally by increasing the intake of certain foods. It is found in unique cells called melanocytes. Inside these melanocytes are vesicles called melanosomes, where tiny granules of the pigment melanin can be found.

Over time, the melanosomes detach themselves from the melanocytes, moving through the body and to other cells, eventually making their way to the epidermal cells. These are the cells found in the two topmost layers of your skin and the concentration and distribution of the melanin pigment determines how light or dark your skin appears. Melanin also absorbs light from a scientific viewpoint, but not in the same way that is known to exist in the cosmos. The darker color absorbs light and protects the DNA of the body from the harmful ultraviolet rays from the sun.

Though melanin exists throughout the body, it is concentrated in several key areas. It is found predominantly in hair, skin, the irises (pupils) of the eyes, the locus coeruleus and substantia nigra of the brain, the stria vascular is of the inner ear, and the zona reticularis and medulla of the adrenal gland. There are three major types of melanin in the body, each playing a specific role.

•	Eumelanin, which is found only in small amounts. These small amounts can do things like make hair blonde in color.

•	Pheomelanin, which is found in the skin and hair. This melanin may give red and pink colors to red-haired people. Though it is darker than eumelanin, it is not as protective against ultraviolet radiation.

- Neuromelanin, which is found throughout the brain. Deficiencies in neuromelanin may cause many types of neurological disorders.

Though you may find scientist who ignore the incredible information that can be derived from an abundance of melanin, it cannot be denied that it exists all in the body of each person on the planet. It is necessary for most bodily functions, comes in three different forms, and must be present to help protect from cancer-causing ultraviolet radiation. The sun is not the enemy of the melanated being.

Melanin on a Cosmic Level

The scientific side of melanin has been established for many years, though for a long time scientists have believed it to be only a pigment to hair and skin color. The truth is that it plays many incredible roles in the body but the scientific definition only begins to scratch the surface. Melanin can also be described as a spiritual energy. It is incredibly powerful because while it can absorb light from all sides of the spectrum, it does not reflect much light. One way to think of melanin is as a partially-charged battery. This battery is always ready to accept and store more electrical charges. These electrical charges are energy, which can be created by focusing on and then storing things like sound and light.

There are four primary types of melanin that exist on a universal level. This includes planetary, cosmic, plant life (in the form of chlorophyll, including fungi and bacteria), and the animal kingdom (which we are a part of). As someone of African descent, you have rich melanin sources that exist in pure to near-pure form. In modern times, the larger amount of melanin found in Africans was not known about until the Vietnam War. When soldiers were killed during the war, they were shipped overseas to America before undergoing an autopsy to determine the cause of death. During these autopsies, the soldiers' brains were dissected. As scientists examined the brain, it was found that the pineal gland found in the brain of a Caucasian person was smaller than the pineal gland found in African soldiers.

Melanin and Ancient Egypt
A highly debated historical topic is what the skin color of Ancient Egyptians was. When people hear the term 'Egyptian,' some project it as a predominantly white society. Even though Egypt exists geographically in Africa, it is commonly believed that Egyptians are white, coming from North and South of the Sahara Desert and

having differing skin tones that were lighter in nature. A major influencer of this opinion was a French scientist, Professor Pierre-Fernand Ceccaldi. In 1975, an unpreserved mummy was uncovered in Egypt. Ramesses II was flown to France, to be preserved by Professor Ceccaldi. The mummy of Ramesses had well-preserved hair, which was reddish in color. It was concluded that Ramesses II was a fair-skinned person that had ginger-colored hair. This discovery of this pigmentation heavily influenced the opinions of many scientists during the time, especially since there was not yet data that could disprove it. However, another theory in 2008 described the Egyptians as an incredibly diverse race, with its inhabitants coming from all over Africa. This would explain why the pigmentation of Ramesses was not representative of the entire race of Ancient Egypt.

Later in the 1970s, a group of scientists developed the Black Egyptian hypothesis. This hypothesis has since been adopted in the Afrocentric belief system, stating that Ancient Egypt was a society predominantly made up of melanated individuals. There are even some modern scholars that recognize this idea to an extent, agreeing that Nubians (indigenous Egyptian) and many Pharaohs had a black ancestral line. However, the beliefs under the

Black Egyptian hypothesis claims that all of Egypt, from the northernmost to the southernmost parts of the country, was a black civilization. It is also believed that there are links to Sub-Saharan cultures that prove this relationship. Additionally, there are many individuals who existed during what is known as the Dynastic time period who were believed to be black, including notable men and women of history, including the inspiration for the Great Sphinx of Giza, King Tutankhamun and Cleopatra.

Today, there are still many scholars who support this idea, including Cheikh Anta Diop, Martin Bernal, Chancellor Williams, W.E.B. Du Bois, Segun Magbagbeola, Ivan van Sertima, and John G. Jackson. These scholars debated with others about the validity of the Black African hypothesis throughout the 20th century, with many of them using the descriptive terms 'Egyptian', 'African', and 'Black' interchangeably in their writing, research, and speech. One of the most influential of these scholars was Cheikh Anta Diop, who used a multi-faceted approach to uncover the truth about the presence or lack thereof of melanin in the Ancient Egyptians. Diop tested skin samples from Egyptian mummies uncovered during the Mariette excavations by putting them under a microscope. Between the dermis and epidermis of the skin, melanin levels were tested, and it was found that they were undeniably black. Diop also tested blood samples, finding that many of them had the 'B' blood type, which is most common in the African race. However, this research was not completely conclusive since the Egyptian samples were all from the same excavation site.

A 2017 study involved the extraction of DNA from 151 mummies of Egypt, uncovered in the Middle Egypt territory of Abusir el-Meleq. The DNA in these mummies were some of the first that were uncontaminated and completely intact. According to the age of the mummies, they lived during the time period of the late New Kingdom and the early Roman era, from the years 1388BCE to 146CE. They were able to uncover complete DNA for 90 of the mummies uncovered, which showed a similar profile during the entire period of time. Additionally, three of the mummies were analyzed to find Y-DNA, which is a common mitochondrial profile for North Africans and Middle Easterners. Even so, this single site still had a limited portrayal of all Ancient Egyptian life.

Another major proponent of this claim that all of Egypt was black is the intelligence of Ancient Egyptians. The Egyptians built the pyramids and are responsible for many of the inventions we have in today's society. Man has learned a lot from the life of the Ancient Egyptian. Many of the scholars supporting the Black Egyptian hypothesis believe they must be black because of the power of melanin. Already, it was known that the melanin that caused darker skin pigmentation did not serve just the purpose of determining skin tone. It was already known that melanin could absorb and exude a creative energy. This is shown through the ancient texts that describe the Egyptian's great machines, as well as their ability to fly in gliders, measure the distance from earth to the sun, and electroplate gold. Many other societies were overshadowed by the Ancient Egyptians as society spread, and the Egyptians became known as masters of magic like remote viewing, psychokinesis, and precognition.

The final factor in the Black Egyptian hypothesis is the belief that all of civilization stemmed from the Ancient Egyptians. It is believed that they were the first human society created. The evidence behind this is the purity of some men and women of African descent. When a person of lighter skin tone has children with someone of a darker skin tone, it is impossible to keep that same purity of melanin. Therefore, it would only make sense that those of African descent were among the first living on earth, thus, the first Egyptians that walked the earth were black.

How Melanin Works as a Creative Power

Have you ever heard of techniques like positive thought or positive visualization? These two techniques require the practicing individual to think about what they wish to bring into existence. They think of how they would like a situation to play out or what desires they have. The creative power of melanin, as you will see as you read through the book, works similar in this way. The abundance of melanin within your being allows you to attract the vibrations from the universe that align with the energy you are putting forth. Imagine for a moment that, you desire inner peace and no longer stimulate from worldly desires. You would send out a positive, high vibration to attract that positive event that will lead to you advancing down that path.

You have probably heard the expression, 'like attracts like.' While this is not always true of people, it is always true of cosmic energy. The thoughts that you have and the way that you put forth your energy in the world attracts whatever you put out. If you continue to think that you will never be successful, that is what is going to happen. Instead, put out the positive vibe that you will find a solution. This solution will attract itself to your vibrational frequencies, bringing the ideas that you create into the physical world.

Chapter 2: The Many Benefits of Melanin

Melanin is the black matter of all that exists. Even in the lightest beings, trace amounts of melanin are at work protecting their eyes and improving brain function. Melanin may even be considered the key to life itself, the solitary chemical involved in our being. Melanin has been found to be present in abundance during the moment of conception and as the embryo develops into what will be a child. This makes it an essential part of our lives, capable of manifesting itself not only on a physical level, but on a spiritual level. There are many benefits of melanin, both for our bodies and our spirits.

Physical Benefits of Melanin

#1: It is Necessary for Embryotic Development
Even from the moment of your conception, the dark matter melanin that is at the center of all in the universe protects you. It encases the egg and

sperm as they join at the moment of conception, keeping them safe. Once you become an embryo, melanin works inside of that embryo, creating the products of the neural crest including nerve cells, brain cells, and melanocytes. When an embryo is formed without enough melanin, it can lead to miscarriage or birth defects.

#2: Melanin Improves Brain Functions
Even when an individual does not possess the type of melanin that colors the skin, the black brain matter that is melanin still exists. This is necessary for primary brain functions, including motivational, emotional, motor, and sensory activities. The greater the amount of melanin within the brain, the greater these (and other creative powers) are.

#3: It Slows the Aging Process
If you have ever compared the skin of an African American against the skin of someone with a lighter complexion of the same age, you may notice that the skin of those of African descent is usually smoother. This is because melanin protects from the damaging effects of UV rays from the sun. This prevents wrinkles and sun damage, promoting smooth, supple skin, even as you age.

#4: Heightened Melanin Levels Are Healing and Preventative

Melanin is a very healing substance, as it promotes cell regeneration and health throughout the body. The way that it protects cells allows it to lower the risk of cancers, especially melanoma. It also helps prevent genetic disorders, especially autoimmune disorders that cause the cells of the body to attack themselves. Finally, melanin repairs damaged tissue and both prevents and fights infections.

#6: It Protects from Damage of the Sun's Rays

Melanated individuals rarely burn from the sun- they simply absorb its energy. People may tan or become darker with sun exposure, which is the result of melanin being absorbed into the skin. People who are melanin recessive, however, may burn from being in the sun. Instead of protecting from damage, their skin reflects the light's rays and absorbs dangerous ultraviolet radiation. This is why it is important for individuals who have not been blessed with an abundance of melanin to use sunscreen and other methods to protect from harmful rays.

#7: Melanin Protects the Eyes

Eyes that are brown or black in color are covered in a coating of melanin. This melanin protects from sun damage, acting as natural sunglasses. When people who do not have melanated eyes look at sunlight, they may experience irritation or damage. Those with hazel, green, or blue eyes can have problems including irritation, burning, discomfort, and even tissue damage.

#8: Your Body Responds to Your Mind More Quickly
Melanin exists in the brain; therefore, it is brain cells. When the same melanin cells found in your brain are present throughout your body, the message of movement can be passed much more quickly. This explains one of the reasons that blacks often excel in sports and dancing. It is because the message to move can be passed more quickly through the body, giving a better response time and improved ability.

Spiritual Benefits of Melanin

#1: It Nourishes All the Cells of Your Being
One of the ways that melanin is charged is by being in the sun. When ultraviolet rays are reflected, the other light from the sun is absorbed through the skin. Here, this light energy becomes a nutrient that feeds all the cells of our body, giving them health and power. You can also create this nutrient by contact with radio waves, music, and cosmic waves. Your body absorbs, stores, and then distributes the

melanin throughout the body, so all the cells can regenerate themselves. Some even say that you do not need to eat food and drink all the time to be healthy- deeply melanized individuals can charge from the sunlight.

#2: Melanin Lets You Emit Your Own Vibrational Frequency
Those with rich melanin stores have been discriminated against for many years, some people blaming distribution or wealth or being different. The truth is that those of African descent are looked at differently because they are different. As a melanated being, your source of creative energy is much greater than that of lesser melanated being. This spurs creative thought and when you have the attitude that you can accomplish, you can put forth the vibrational frequency that will determine what you receive from the world.

#3: You Can Learn to Be True to Yourself
Those who embrace melanin most effectively do so by aligning it with their values. They learn what they desire most and how they want to use this energy to create goodness in their lives. When you choose to acknowledge the power of melanin, you are reversing oppression. You learn to hold true to your values and then to work for the greater good in your life, regardless of if

someone is willing to provide opportunity or not. When you embrace your melanin origins, you open the door to the universe and the physical world will no longer stand in your way.

#4: You Will Not Die with Regrets
You and you alone have the power to decide what to do with the knowledge that you will learn as you continue in this world. Melanin often gives those in tune with it great and powerful ideas. When you use these ideas, they become your reality. You will live at peace, instead of with the guilt that you never put your great ideas into motion. You will be remembered, rather than leaving the world with just thoughts of what you could have been.

#5: You Become Free
Finally, when you begin to embrace your melanin on a spiritual level, you begin to free yourself. Through centuries of history, the African population has been seen as the lesser species. They have been oppressed and taken advantage of, simply because other racial groups were frightened of what would happen should the African race realize their true potential. When you do realize this potential, you become free. By realizing that you are deeply connected with the cosmos and that you do not have to be a

victim to the oppression that surrounds you, you liberate yourself and liberate your soul.

These suppressed truths are just some of the knowledge that melanin is capable of, on a physical and spiritual level. As you read, think about how the different steps will bring these benefits into your life. Realize these benefits and put your plans into action.

Chapter 3: The Presence of Melanin on a Spiritual Level

It is true that the physical presence of melanin in your being presents immediate benefits, such as protecting the tissues of your skin, eyes, and cells. However, the melanin that exists within those of African descent on a spiritual level is much more advanced. It is this melanin of your spirit that has the potential to change your entire life.

The Direct Relationship Between Skin Pigmentation and Brain Cells
Before the embryo becomes a fetus, the outer layer of skin (the ectoderm) produces melanin.

This melanin eventually helps grow into the brain, as it has 12 melanated centers which are known as black nuclei. The outer layer they grow in (the blastula) becomes the spinal cord and eventually the brain. The twelfth nuclei is considered the highest. This is the nuclei that will begin to form the brain, known as the locus coeruleus.

It is believed that the locus coeruleus is the closest human connection to spirituality and an altered state of consciousness. This is also the area of the mind that allows humans to access the dream world. It is believed that this dream world allows us to learn from our past ancestors, that we can channel the creative powers of those of African descent who have walked the earth. Though we are both part of the animal kingdom, animals typically have a lighter pigment than those of African descent. Less of them have pigmented 'centers' in their mind, thus, they will not all be able to reach the same level of consciousness that humans can.

The chlorophyll of plants also has a similarity to the spiritual melanin of a human. The melanin within you always seeks greatness and is only held back by the limitations that you put on it. Plants take in their melanin as sun also, using it for food to promote growth. As a plant grows, it often grows toward the sunlight of the earth, finding the best, brightest food source and reaching toward it. As human beings, our melanin content can also motivate us to reach to higher developed states of consciousness, learning what our true values are and then using the power of melanin to manifest our desires in the world.

The Spiritual Beliefs of Early African Scientists

Before the time of oppression, African scientists realized the incredible connection between the melanin of their skin and the melanin of their mind. It was believed that the connection of carbon and black melanin life force, was divine, for it was within all things that inhabit the earth. Ancient Africans often called themselves various names that meant black, like 'Kemites', which means people of the black earth. Scientists of the time worked hard to uncover the secret inner workings of their mind, understanding the relationship between the mind and body. Eventually, these scientists learned that the level of 'blackness' of the skin was directly related to a higher level of spirituality and inner vision. Those who realized this connection realized the divine presence within them. They realized the vibratory energies that swirled around them, all the different shades of black that existed as the color of the ocean of outer space that is the universe. The dark matter is the birthplace of all the planets in the solar system, the stars in the sky, all the galaxies in the universe, and all the living and non-living things that exist in the cosmos. The purest presence of this carbon, this black matter, is the black holes that are scattered across the universe. These black holes are the richest source of carbon in the universe, as all they do is absorb all energy that comes into their path.

The role of carbon in all this has to do with the chemical form of melanin. Melanin can be thought of as a chain of carbon atoms that have lined together. These incredible chemical captures light and has the potential to reproduce itself. Within the brain, black neuromelanin is the core of what is responsible for inner vision and intuition. It is also responsible for one's spiritual illumination and creative genius. The reason that melanin opens all these pathways is because it allows you access to the inner workings of the subconscious mind. Within the subconscious mind lies the wisdom of your ancestors, like a timeless memory bank that has collected all the information learned by the knowledgeable, creative Africans that have walked this earth and learned to harness their incredible spiritual energy.

One of many great scientists discussed was George Washington Carver. Carver is credited with discovering the many uses of the peanut, but there is more to his story. Some scholars believe that it was not his Master's Degree in Chemistry that allowed him to come up with all his original genius ideas, but the knowledge of self they drove his discoveries... George Washington Carver was very dark in nature and had an incredible mind, one that was open and receptive to the creative genius of the black melanin of his brain. Carver was noted to take early morning strolls, which he believed fostered an environment to absorb sunlight and clear his conscious, which guided him to take the next step in his research. The problem with this theory was the effect that it had on African American children, who began to resist traditional teaching methods because they desired to be in tune with nature and preferred to learn outside.

Your Melanin Gives You the Power to Control Your Vibrational Frequency

Melanin has the power to absorb and to put forth. As you charge your melanin, you give it greater power. However, you should not confuse this great power with getting what you want. The vibrational frequency put forth from your melanin has the potential to be positive or negative. It is what you choose to consciously do with this power that will go out into the world. As you create this vibrational frequency, that which is similar will come to you in abundance.

Create a high vibrational frequency, refusing to let negative thoughts and excessive worry into your mind. When you emit this high frequency of melanin, it attracts other high frequencies. This is because whatever you choose to resonate as your own energy, you attract. This works similar to the way that glass breaks when a high note is sung.

Many people believe that breaking a glass with a high note is a parlor trick of sorts. However, there is a science behind the way that it works. Think for a moment of the sound that a glass makes when a small metal tine is struck against it to make a sound. Imagine this as a chord. When the note carried from the vocal chords of the singer reach the same frequency of the glass, it breaks. The energy in this scenario starts in the singer's vocal chords, traveling across as a sound. Then, the energy is pushed into the air of the throat before being pushed out through the mouth and into the surrounding area. This energy then moves through the air, being attracted to the glass. As it starts to equal the energy of the glass, the two sounds resonate as one. This creates a great vibration, one that moves through the glass. When the glass can contain no more energy, the vibration is strong enough that the glass breaks.

Melanin and Race

When most people think of the first people on the earth, especially those who follow the Bible, they think of Adam and Eve. Though the skin color of these 'first people' has never been scientifically examined, it is commonly believed that they were white. However, if the first people were white, how could they create a melanated being? While people with lower levels of melanin can seek sunlight and attract more melanin, this will eventually fade with time. Even if it is maintained, a person with this low level of melanin could never become as dark as those of true African descent. It would make sense, therefore, that Africans were the first beings. As people with melanin deficiencies bore children that were lighter, other races were created from the African race. Migration to different areas, farther away from the equator, also played a role in the lighter skin tones that would contribute to future races. This is one of the things that makes those of African descent so incredible on a spiritual level. All races, those of brown, yellow, and white skin tones, are derived from this original African race. It is impossible to create someone of pure African descent from all the less-melanated races of the world, but it is possible to derive all the different melanin states from an African bloodline. In some people with a lighter complexion, there melanin appears as clusters of freckles on areas of the body that get the most natural sun exposure.

The Four Categories of Race
Scientists who have studied how melanin relates to race from a cosmic perspective have classified humans into four groups according to the amount of melanin contained within their body and the spectrum of light that can be absorbed as a result. To understand this, remember that melanosomes are tiny pockets in which the potential (or lack of potential) of the body to create melanin lies.

Stage 1: Someone with Stage 1 melanin levels has empty melanosomes. They do not possess the necessary equipment to make melanin. These types of people maybe melanin recessive and may need to adjust their diet or increase sun exposure to remain healthy.

Stage 2: A person with Stage 2 melanin levels has the ability to make melanin. Their body has plenty of potential, but the melanosomes themselves are empty of melanin.

Stage 3: An individual with Stage 3 has access to some of their melanin, as they possess the machinery to create melanin and also have melanosomes that are filled half-way with melanin.

Stage 4: At this stage, the individual likely has a dark complexion. Their body possess the necessary machinery to make melanin and also has melanosomes that are completely filled with melanin.

People of Caucasian descent have Stages 1 and 2. While they all possess melanin to an extent, they do not necessarily possess the melanin levels necessary to connect on a spiritual level. It is common for people of Asian, Latino, and Hispanic descent to be Stage 3, with skin tones that are not light but that contain at least some degree of melanin. Those of African descent are common to Stages 3 and 4, depending on the purity of the melanin within. Regardless, Stages 3 and 4 have the most potential for connecting to the universe on a cosmic level and bringing your great ideas and your deepest desires into existence in the physical world. People of color also have circulating melanin, which is caused when excess melanin spills from the melanosomes into the blood and circulates through the body. In a way, those like albino people who may be melanin recessive, may even be seen as having a genetic disorder.

Racial Background and Energy Absorption

We see the color of those around us as we would everyday objects. The light is absorbed or reflected off of the individual's skin, depending on their melanin content. Skin color, therefore, is a matter of perception, but melanin content is not. The amount of melanin within your skin determines the range of light energy that can be absorbed. Those with Stage 4 melanin can absorb the entire light spectrum, from basic electric power to the great cosmic waves. Those with Stage 1 melanin can absorb a very limited amount of the light spectrum, which means they must intake their melanin from other sources. They also cannot absorb this wide range of energy that connects melanted beings to the cosmos.

Hyper Perception

Melanin is highly integrated in the nervous system of African American human beings. This nervous system is what is responsible for perceiving the world around us. It is what gives us the ability to perceive what we see, smell, taste, feel, and hear. We interpret these things and they become reality. Since those of African descent have such a connection between their mind and their skin, it is almost as if there is a second brain that grows on the outside of the body. It is this brain that perceives the world around you when you are of African descent, allowing you to be aware of all your surroundings. When you are in tune with this 'outer' brain, you become that much closer to the people and things around you. This means that as you experience life, you have a closer, more human experience because you can perceive all things.

Melanin and the Cosmos: An Example

One highly studied group of Africans during ancient times is the Dogon Tribe of Mali. These African people have very deep melanin skin tones, so it would stand that they would be a Stage 4 level of melanin and have the ability to the entire universal energy spectrum.

The reason the Dogon people are so interesting is because they have explored the universe and uncovered and recorded intricate details of the cosmos beyond us, even before man went into space.

Some of the details they uncovered include where our star (the sun) lies, where the white dwarf companion of Sirius exists in the sky, the rings of Saturn, how the milky way has a spiral structure, and the moons of Jupiter. Even though you cannot see these things with the human eye, the Dogon tribe was able to observe and record them. The Dogons also uncovered them before the time of technological instruments. So, the question remains, how?

The Dogons relied on their existence as melanated beings. They were able to sense these astrological patterns, making record of them as drawing on their clothing and the huts that they lived in. This mystery plagued the Europeans in the years to come, especially since at the time this Dogon information was uncovered the Europeans had just started to uncover these cosmic entities- and that was only with the help of high-powered telescopes! The Dogons felt the existence of these cosmic entities, perceiving them with their second mind and recording this information as reality. This is something that would never be possible for someone who was melanin recessive.

Another example of this incredible power of melanin is the way that Ancient Africans communicated. There is a reason that Africans today are so incredible at the drum, especially tribes living within third-world countries. The drums are a means of communications. Ancient Africans could send these sounds and images using the drum, communicating with tribes who were hundreds of miles away from the source of the drumming.

If you compare the abilities of the Dogons and other African tribes of the time against the Europeans, it becomes clear that there is a major difference in their abilities to perceive the universe and use it for their understanding and advancement. This difference is not in the civilization or the access of materials, but in the ability of blacks to harness the ability of melanin on a cosmic level and use it for greatness.

African Hair, the Golden Spiral, and the Electricity of Melanin

The hair of those of African descent is also incredibly powerful, with its spirals and its ability to attract and store electricity giving those who wear it incredible potential.

The Golden Spiral

The spiral is something that can be seen through all of creation. The Golden Spiral is a symbol highly valued in the universe. It is said that all life is created of a spectrum of circles, each of these being weaved throughout one another.

This spiral is found in birth and death, with every breath in and out, and in the differing worlds of day and night. It is often called the 'Divine Proportion', as this spiral and its constant can be found throughout the universe. It is present in the spirals of your fingertips and the shape of the human ear, as well as in the waves of the ocean, the double helix of the DNA molecule of all living things on the universe, the shape that roots and stems follow as they extend from seeds, in seashells, and in all other things in the universe.

Every human being has these swirls on their heads, as even Caucasians have a whorl pattern from which hair sprouts on their head. However, those with straight hair have only this pattern, which comes to an end at the roots of their hair. As someone of African descent, your spirals extend beyond this initial whorl and into your hair. The longer your hair is, the more creative power you hold within it.

The Electricity of African Hair
When people think of 'African' hair, they often think of hair that is dark in color, wavy, thick, nappy, and frizzy. This hair can be incredibly difficult to manage, as it seems to always be electrified and wanting to reach toward the skies. However, this is not necessarily a bad thing.

Have you ever appreciated your hair for what it truly was? It is not uncommon for men and women of African descent to wish they had more manageable hair, some of them even resorting to dying it, straightening it, and making it lie flat. When you make your hair lie flat, you are stopping your flow of power. When you dye your hair, you are taking away from its ability to absorb and attract all the electricity from the different spectrums of universal light. When you tamper with your true African hair, you are tampering with your ability to absorb and digest information from the sun.

Often, it is taught that true beauty is to have smooth, sleek, and beautiful hair. It is taught that lighter, fairer skin is beautiful. However, all is beautiful. This is a trick that diminishes what you truly are, by depleting your access to the great dark matter that covers the cosmos. Allow your hair to grow naturally. Style it, but do not use relaxers and other harmful ingredients that take away from the majestic being that you truly are. Learn to embrace your hair and value it for the incredible way that it pulls melanin and the creative power of the universe into your field so that you may shape it, project it, and bring the things that you desire into reality.

Chapter 4: Boosting Melanin Levels: What to Do and What to Avoid

It is true that we are born with melanin. This dark matter is our beginning and as someone of African descent, it is a gift to you in your life. It gives you the power of smooth, simple skin, the power of creative intelligence, and the power of directing energy so that you may choose what to attract in your life. However, when this black matter is neglected or avoided, it goes to waste. As you will read, you will learn the things that you should and should not do- to improve melanin levels and maximize your abilities and to prevent activities that deplete the melanin stores and the power you hold within.

What You Can Do: Improve Tyrosine Levels
Tyrosine has a profound effect on how much melanin is present in the body. In fact, tyrosine is known to cause albinism (white, colorless skin and sometimes red irises) when it is deficient. This means that when your body does not produce, or you do not consume enough tyrosine, it depletes your stores of melanin and decreases your power. Even though tyrosine is an amino acid naturally produced by the body,

sometimes the body's stores are not enough. There are three ways to boost tyrosine levels.

First, you can increase your intake of certain foods that have high concentrations of tyrosine. This includes seaweed, pumpkin flesh, mustard greens, cottage cheese, egg whites, tuna, kidney beans, sesame seeds, cod, avocado, spinach, and bananas. Eating a variety of these types of food is sufficient for some people, especially those who regularly include these in their diet.

The second option is dietary powders or supplements. When you consume food sources of tyrosine, it will not all remain after the digestive process. Additionally, tyrosine is difficult to pass through the blood-brain barrier. When you choose to supplement with tyrosine, it is often in a form that is easily digested by the body. You also have the advantage of knowing how much tyrosine you are taking.

Finally, you can consume foods or supplement with phenylalanine. Phenylalanine is the precursor to tyrosine, meaning that the body makes tyrosine from phenylalanine. It is also absorbed much easier through the blood-brain barrier, so it is more accessible to your body. You can supplement phenylalanine with a capsule or powder, or you can get it from your diet. Some good sources of this amino acid include fish (including crab, cod, catfish, tuna, sardines, lobster, oysters, and mussels), which has an entire day's requirement in a portion, meats including chicken, turkey, beef, and liver, gelatin, eggs, dairy products including cheese, milk, and cream cheese, nuts, legumes like lentils and chickpeas, soy products, and aspartame.

What You Can Do: Recharging Your Melanin in Your Daily Life

In addition to taking in melanin using dietary means, it is important that you recharge your melanin naturally as well. Doing things like being out in the sun, early morning walks, or moving through dance are just some of the ways that you can recharge your solar power. It is also important to get enough sleep. It is shown that the pineal gland is most active between the hours of 11 p.m. and 7 a.m., though it is only active while the mind is asleep. Get as much sleep as you can during this time to encourage the natural production of melanin. Sleeping during this time is also said to be the most enlightening, since it is the pineal gland that can open the mind to the world of the unconsciousness and even encourage lucid dreaming.

Sun exposure is highly recommended, to help you boost melanin and absorb the creative energies of the universe. Seek sunlight as often as you can. This will boost your immune system, as well as improve emotional and mental health. It is recommended that melanated individuals get at least 30 minutes of direct sunlight at least three times each week.

Preserving Melanin: What Not To Do

Just as you must encourage melanin production in your body, there are certain things that should be avoided to ensure your pineal gland and melanin are at their fullest capabilities. Here is what you need to know:

- Avoid fluoridated water- Most cities treat their water with fluoride, even though it has been proven to have some adverse health effects. One of these effects is calcification of the pineal gland, which minimizes its capability and power. Avoid city water to prevent this calcification. Do not worry if you have been drinking or cooking with fluoridated water- just stop immediately. You can decalcify it to re-open the pineal gland by using detoxifiers like ginseng, Bentonite clay, chlorophyll, and blue-green algae or by consuming detoxifying foods like seaweed, cilantro, bananas, coconut oil, honey, and watermelon.

- Do not take Vitamin-D supplements- Vitamin D supplements can be dangerous for melanated individuals, especially if you follow the recommended guidelines for getting enough sun each week. Do this naturally instead of supplementing, as the body naturally produces Vitamin D from exposure to the sun. If you are melanin recessive, you may need to supplement but it is still recommended that cod liver oil be used rather than Vitamin D. Vitamin D is hard to absorb, while cod liver oil is easier to absorb and promotes the natural production of Vitamin D by the body.

- Avoid fatty foods- Melanin bonds with fatty compounds, which has two effects. First, it can make you gain weight more easily than someone with less melanin would. Second, it traps your melanin and lessens your ability to harness its power. For this reason, avoid animal fats, saturated fats, and vegetable oils. Instead of choosing vegetable oils, consider those rich in Omega-3s like coconut oil, olive oil, or grapeseed oil.

Chapter 5: Your Responsibility to Harness Your Abilities from Melanin

Stop for a moment think of how you are living your life. How are people going to remember you when you are dead and gone? Will anyone but your family know your name? Will you have made an impact on the people of the world? As an intelligent being, you have a responsibility to ensure that you when you are lying on your deathbed, people are remembering your legacy. By reading this book and learning of the incredible life you are blessed to experience, you place yourself in the footsteps of your ancestors. This debt is the debt of doing what you can to lie the foundation for the future- to be a part of the great change that will occur in the world when knowledge of self is restored.

Your Responsibility: What You Owe the World

There is not any single physical thing or gift that you can give the world for it to suffice as your mark on the world. That which you owe the world is not a physical thing, but the use of your free will. Your responsibility is to use your knowledge for the greater good. We are creatures of light, love, and peace.

When you die, there are two possible scenarios. In the first, you are remembered by all those that love you. They are not sad merely because your physical body is passing on, but because they remember all that you have done in life. They are remembering how you have used your own intellectual wealth and the power that comes along with it to help those that you could. They are remembering all the great ideas that have flowed forth from your mind and all the memorable words that you have given. They are remembering how great you are and how all the world will be at a loss once you have breathed your last breath.

The second scenario is a sad one. You may still be surrounded with those that love you, but you will not see them. Instead, you are going to see all the ideas that you had surrounding you. You are going to see all the things that you wish you had said and wish you had done to leave an impact on the world. In this scenario, your room is full of all the ifs of your life. It is full of all the things that could have been. It is full of those kids who may have tried harder, had you shared your story or those people who were not helped by the incredible ideas that you kept into your head, because you always thought there would be more time.

There is no single place on earth that is wealthier than the graveyard. The graveyard is filled with the unlimited potential of all the people who have been laid to rest without leaving their mark on the world. It is filled with the unrealized dreams of all that lie there, of the speeches that were never given and the inventions that were never created because the person lying in that graveyard believed they had more time.

Your responsibility to the world is to stop holding back. Stop letting races that believe they are greater than you tell you that you are not enough. Stop letting people tell you that you cannot go further, or you cannot embrace your dreams, because you are not good enough or smart enough or strong enough. Refuse to accept the lie pushed onto those of the African race; the lie that you must wait for others to open doors for you before you can realize your dreams. You are enough, and you will be enough, regardless of what others think or say. The power of melanin has been hidden for a long time, but it is time for it to be realized. It is time for people rich in this black, creative matter of the universe to step forth and start making the changes that are necessary in the world.

Stop Now and Realize This

The few paragraphs that follow are among the most important in this book. Read these and know that they are the truth. Read these and feel the power flow through you. Feel the melanin express in your being and experience it as you never have before. Think of all your ideas and your thoughts that you may have wanted to imprint on the world but didn't, because you did not think anyone would listen or because you thought that it was not your place. Perhaps you lacked the motivation and energy. Realize the following words and know that you do have the power to change the world, as soon as you start to take advantage of the benefits embedded in your mind.

People of African descent have the power of melanin in every single cellular structure that exists in our being. It makes up our bodies and it flows through our blood. Melanin is condensed sunlight, full of intelligent information. By refusing to realize and use this gift, we allow the world around us to put us under their oppression. The oppression we face in our lives comes from external sources, but we have the power of deciding if we want to accept it. When you let the negative energy around you shape who you are, it acts as an oppressive force and you respond by limiting yourself. Instead of creating yourself out of the creative intelligence and brilliance that lives within your melanated mind, you create yourself in their oppressive image. In this way, you defeat yourself.

Make the decision to stop this oppression. Make the decision to create your own energy frequency. Do not create energies based on what you are told you may have, but rather what you want. Create your own frequency and then create your own energy. Project the positive mindset and become who you were meant to be from that moment of conception in your life. It is when you make this decision, the decision to become who you were meant to be and to start imparting your unique energy and your love in the world around you, that you can change the world. You must use your intellectual wisdom to do great things, using this wisdom and your creativity in conjunction with the power of free will, you can reach that higher frequency.

To operate on this higher frequency, you must shut out the world and become who you are within. Refuse to live in menial environments and accept less than what you deserve. Raise your expectations and raise your frequency and watch as the universe comes to your beckoning. Watch as the universe responds to this higher frequency and responds to your desires, changing the world around you. Do this for yourself and then do this for your people, demanding what you deserve from life and make change.

As you do this, remember. It is a lie that you are inferior. It is a lie that you must wait around to be handed things and that you must wait for doors to be opened for you. Know that the melanin that flows through your blood and fills every cell of your body is chemical evidence of your greatness. Acknowledge its presence, and embrace. Take complete advantage of it and know that with your conscious, you can create the reality of your world.

Understanding and Overcoming Racism

It has been proven time and time again that as children, we are born without hate. Children and animals in infancy, from that first breath on the planet, hate no one and no thing. Racism, therefore, is a learned thing. Or is it? Why is it that so many people are willing to hate?

While racism is learned, it is also something that has been ingrained in history. As humans have evolved, so have our brains. Even so, there is an ancient part of the brain, the oldest part that exists, that is designed specifically for survival. It is this part of the brain that is required to detect anything that is potentially dangerous or that seems off. When detected, the mind creates a fight-or-flight reaction by pumping hormones like adrenaline and cortisol through the body. While the mind has evolved, this part of the brain exists. It hides, lurking in the depths, but still sometimes affecting what goes on in the subconscious mind. It is by understanding this ancient part of the brain that you can begin to understand the racism that exists in the world and why.

Do you remember the Dogon Tribe of Mali and the Europeans that existed not long after? Do you remember how much more advanced the Dogons were, knowing of things that the Egyptians had only just started to explore? This incredible knowledge that was so advanced for their time period that it could only be inferred that they were superior. Unfortunately, instead of seeking to learn from the intellectual power and creative prowess of the blacks, other societies tried to oppress it. They were not impressed by it, but terrified, terrified of what melanated beings could do if they chose to stand together as one.

The outward hostility that whites show toward blacks goes beyond that of a fear of losing wealth. It is theorized that whites may act this way because of their wealth and their interest in protecting their own wealth, but this is not the case. This racism has been deeply ingrained in the most ancient part of the mind out of fear. Early people knew that blacks were the creator of the other races, that it was the pigment, the melanin that gave them their power. They knew that our genetic makeup was different and that it was dominant, that it was our pigment that would shine through should we make children with someone of a lighter pigment. Once it was uncovered that the existence of melanin was greater in those of African descent and that melanin plays both biological and cosmic roles in the universe, it is no surprise that this greatness was oppressed. It is this melanin, not because of our skin color, but because of our minds, that is the greatest secret.

Fight-or-Flight and Africanism

People who argue against oppression may point to celebrities or politicians that are African as examples of success, but these examples have many layers to them. The elite societies do not fear people of color rising to positions of power or being given opportunities, because they still are not united as a whole, in addition our history is scattered about the Earth. The true root of the fear is that melanated beings will discover their true selves. In the times of White supremacy, blacks were robbed of their identity. They were dictated as to what they should do, how it should be done, and even who they should be as a person. By accepting this as our history and by continuing to remain ignorant of our origins, we continue to be subservient to a supremacist idea. Even though we are past the time of slavery, blacks are still enslaved because they adhere to the labels and guidelines that have been forced upon them by society. In other words, defeat the system, by rising above the system. Empower your mind, and spread knowledge and love throughout the universe

These guidelines were put into place for a reason- Make no mistake your true identity has been hidden. However, the second that we begin to understand ourselves, our relation to the universe, the creative and intellectual power that exists within us, we begin to heighten our conscious. People will emit negative energy regardless. They may tell you to limit yourself or be reserved in your actions. Do not stop. Refuse to let your creations go un-invented and refuse to let your words go unheard. Create and speak. Remember that you are powerful beings of the cosmos.

The Incredulity of Your Being

The first step in realizing our incredulity, of realizing the potential that we have, is realizing how unique we truly are. Consider the structure of your cellular body. Did you know that every second you are alive, your body replaces 10 million of these melanin-rich cells, with stronger, healthier replacements for the old cells? Within three months, every single cell that makes up your current structural being will be gone but you will still exist. This is because you are made of a supreme intelligent design. Even with evolution and your ever-changing body, you remain uniquely you. Your form is not randomly acquired; therefore, your existence is not a mere mistake. It happened for a reason and by refusing to seek to learn that reason and refusing to learn what impact it is you can make on the world, you are cheating yourself and all those who sacrificed before you, who walk beside you, and who will walk after you. There is no thing or creation or event in this world that is accidental. There is not a single thing that happens just because. Cause and effect is always at play. The moment you realize this, you will stop becoming the effect and you will start creating the cause. As you do this, you become the cause in your life and what you reap as a result becomes the effects. Step into the role of your design and begin to act as a person fulfilling that design should act.

The evidence of your greatness is all around you. Look around at the people who have adapted your culture. Look at the music, foods, inventions, and culture that were wholly African but that have been adopted by other cultures, without the slightest acknowledgement. Know this occurs because they are attracted to your frequency. Know that this is your greatness and continue to strive. Strive first as an individual and then as a group, using your thoughts and creations and those thoughts and creations of other spiritual beings to assure your rightful place in the world at last.

The final thing that you must remember, as you go onto become all that you are capable of, is that even with higher knowledge comes responsibility. Do not try to take from or oppress others on your quest to greatness. Know that as you interact, we are all different but important. No person is superior, but we should all have our rights to succeed and excel in this world. Simply refuse to accept any label that is pushed upon you. Do not accept the mediocracy or the 'just living' that is afforded to you. Instead, use the vibrational energy that has been gifted to you since the moment of your creation to branch out and create your own reality.

Chapter 6: Techniques You Can Use to Harness the Energy of Melanin

Up to this point, you have learned what melanin is, what it can do, how to use its energy responsibly, and how to best maintain the melanin levels in your body- but how do you use it? This chapter will teach you exactly what you need to know to start using all this energy that has been absorbed in the melanosomes of your body.

Step 1: Foster a Positive Mindset
Positivity is the first essential element of using the melanin in our lives. Do not mistake melanin for this great force that will create great things in your life regardless of what you put into it. Melanin does create, but it can create both positive and negative. For this reason, start each day with a positive mindset.

The first thing that you should do is called priming. Priming is an exercise that helps you reach an optimal state in your mind, one that is prepared to send out positive vibrational energies. This is important because if you let negative thoughts creep into your mind and bring you down, you bring your vibrational frequencies down. This can attract undesirable or even unpleasant things from the world around you, since the energy you emit creates your reality. If you act and think as if you are helpless, what the universe will deliver you is helplessness. The way to overcome this is to focus on your creative and positive energies, feeling confident that you can create the solution to any problem you may come across. Always start the day by clearing your mind of any negative thoughts. Avoid complaining, verbally acknowledge the good. If you do hear negative thoughts, release them from your mind. Assure yourself that a solution is available and return to the positive.

The second thing you should do is create a mindset of gratitude. Be thankful for what you do have. The reason that this is so important is because without an attitude of gratefulness for what you already have, you cannot be happy. Without happiness, you cannot possibly have a positive mindset. Create a list of at least 5 things that you are grateful for and take a moment to relish in them, being appreciative that you have each in your life.

Step 2: Block Out Negativity

It is true you cannot always control the world around you. You cannot control that your company is laying people off or that you were cut off in traffic. What you can control, however, is how you react to these things. Negative thoughts are sure to creep into your mind as you go about your day, especially if you get bad news or find yourself faced with an obstacle. In these times, you must block out the negativity and remember that the solution is available. Trust in your instincts, and that creative power that resides in yourself. Push any negative thoughts you may be having from your mind. As you do, affirm that you will be okay. Affirm that regardless of what the future holds, you will find the solution that once again propels you to the top. Embrace the Yin and Yang.

Step 3: Envisioning Your Desires

When you imagine something, you bring it that much closer into being. Over the last decade, many studies have been done that researched the pathways of the brain and how they light up during certain activities. Several studies have found that imagining something in full detail lights up the same pathways that would be created if you were actually having that experience. The mind cannot tell whether it is creating a scenario or living it. This brings you closer to your desires, as your mind guides you to think and act in a way that attracts that scenario to your life.

As you envision what it is you want, choose an area where you can completely focus. Think of the scenario with as much detail as you can, from the way that your date's perfume/cologne smells to the way you will shake your client's hand before the presentation. Think of each detail and then re-play this scenario, again and again, until it becomes the truth in your life.

Step 4: Listen to the Melanin Within

You cannot expect that which you want most to happen overnight, nor without you putting in the work. Continue to create a positive attitude and learn to listen to the flow of your melanin. When you have a creative thought, embrace it, instead of pushing it away. When you have a great idea and your conscious mind pushes you to be quiet, because you think you will be shunned, speak it anyway. Learn to go with the flow of your life and remain open to what your life force may be guiding you to do. It is in this way that you will realize what you can do to help promote your own life and the lives of others.

Step 5: Remember to Recharge Your Melanin

As you embrace higher self, and give conscious to your energy, you must remember to recharge it. Otherwise, you will find that your motivation dwindles away. You may also find that you feel weaker and even experience illness more often. Go out in the sun often and seek out other forms of light to absorb. Dance to music, create your own rhythm, and remember to get a full night of sleep. Do all those things that your body needs so that as you realize the things you want in your life, you remain healthy enough and strong enough to seek them.

Spiritual Immune System

The Spiritual Immune System:

Your spiritual immune system in a sense, is metaphysically operating in the same ways or functions that your physical immune system operates.

What do I mean by this?

To strengthen your immune system, your immune system has to become diagnosed with the outside entity, or sickness, in this case that it is trying to strengthen itself from.

For example, you have individuals who catch a common cold and stand a good chance of dying do to never being exposed to such elements. This is how many of the Native Americana died. Europeans had many pathogens and zoonotic diseases from living among animals, that when they came to America the immune system of the indigenous people in America was compromised. This is how great populations were wiped out when it comes to hygiene and disease.

Science of the immune system:

In many historic tribes, the practice of introducing a minimal amount of snake venom to the child was practiced to build up the child's immune system to the threats of the wild.

You can develop your immune system and condition your body to combat anything that can be entered into it.

It is called genetic conditioning. When speaking on the biological immune system, we want to take the same understanding of how that immune system operates and apply it to the spiritual immune system. in order to strengthen the spiritual immune system, you have to experience life. This is the importance of growth.

you need to develop a higher capacity of expression. When you examine life at a youthful age you're not even able to conceive advanced methods of expressing yourself, you usually go with the path of least resistance, anger.

Take an example from infancy to five years old, you can only express a limited amount of emotion. From ages five to ten your level of creativity has heightened to where instead of verbally expressing what you feel inside, you now might be able to draw, or paint, even poetry.
Fast forwarding from ten to adulthood, you are capable to create a form of communicating higher-level thoughts. The point of growth is for you to constantly express your internal energy, adapt and overcome. When your body grows it increases your strength and functionality, life experience is what will forge your inner spirit, which connects to all.

Take this understanding and look at your immune system, many are operating outside the concept of Oneness, the cosmic completeness, the universe. When one does this, they are living inside individual egotistical disguises.

Everyone produces an aura known as the electromagnetic field. People will alter your aura on the level of frequency through thought and energetic projection, in this form we call it emotion, emotion stands for energy in motion.

When we address the spiritual immune system those who are sensitive to energetic attacks, have not yet developed a higher spiritual immune system. Building your spiritual immune system does not mean volunteering for rough situations in life and hoping to come out stronger, that could be mistaken for stupidity.

Building your spiritual immune system is focused on when outside entities introduce themselves to you and you develop the capacity to combat that entity. Spiritually you guide yourself mentally, so whatever negative entity attacks your spiritual immune system, the answer is to use your knowledge you have available to you. In other words when you heal from a sickness you are now immune to its future attacks.

In your physical immune system, disease starts at: 50 megahertz or below as we are electrical beings. When you eat electrically charged foods you keep your body vibrating on a higher frequency which can prevent many common disease.

Conclusion

Through our lives, we are often taught that to succeed, we must work twice as hard. We are taught that we are supposed to live a "certain" lifestyle and conform to society. The true power begins when knowledge of self is achieved.

As melanated beings, we are powerful. Every core of our being is made up of melanin, the dark matter that exists in every living and nonliving being of the universe. We must learn to embrace this energy and to focus our will that thrives within us to create our own vibrational energies in the universe. Through the creation of these energies, we can achieve greatness and ascend into higher consciousness.

Stop allowing outside forces to oppress you. Learn to embrace your melanated nature. Never feel ashamed of your natural skin, hair and power. Your thoughts are powerful enough to manifest the reality around you, think of yourself in the highest regards.

Always seek to absorb the sun so that your melanosomes are filled as much as sunlight as possible. Seek out the sun so you may recharge and vibrate on a positive frequency. Find the energy sources that you thrive on and seek them as often as possible. Use this to broadcast your own frequency and bring what it is that you want into being. Understand your nature and the truth of your being and allow this to bring what it is that you desire most in the world. Resist all the negative imprints of the world around you and understand that you operate at a level intimidating to others. Use this knowledge not to seek control or to destroy others, but to create a reality unlike one that you have ever imagined. Remember that you are light, love, and peace. Whenever you need to be reminded of your true essence, simply stand in the sun.

As you embark on your journey of self-discovery, remember to use your energy in a way that would pride your ancestors and in a way that will benefit future generations. Never accept false pretenses- raise your standards and strive to spread your ideas and your messages until it becomes the truth of the world. You and you alone have the power to create your own reality.

Made in the USA
Columbia, SC
27 April 2019